For all pets
you've loved and
lost.
warm regards
Mary McMillan

Cold Wet Noses

Whiskers

And

Tweets

Poems by
Marjorie C. Mc Millan, DVM

Cover Design and Photography by
Joan Powers

First printing, 2017
ISBN-13: -978-1973938842
ISBN-10: 1973938847

Dedicated to Sterling, Norman, and Eleanor, my
greatest teachers, whose fur and feathers filled my life
with joy and live eternally in my heart

INTRODUCTION

This collection of poems will make you laugh, will make you cry but mostly it will capture your heart. It is a tribute to my patients who have always captured my heart and break my heart when they die. I hope their humans can find comfort in the sad poems and laughter in the more humorous ones. Inspiration for my poetry comes from my daily work with animals and long walks in the forest observing the woodland critters and the changing landscape of the seasons.

From the time I could say the word animal doctor at about three years old I wanted to be a veterinarian. It is a gift to be able to work with animals each day and make them feel better through kind and compassionate care and return them healthier to their families.

Veterinary medicine for all its rewards can be emotionally challenging. Veterinarians have four times the suicide rate of the general population and poetry allows me to channel the difficult emotions into a creative process that honors the work that I do and the animals I treat.

This collection celebrates the twenty-fifth anniversary of my clinic, The Windhover Veterinary Center, named after a poem by Gerard Manley Hopkins.

Marjorie C. Mc Millan

Table of Contents

Cold wet noses, whiskers and tweets

Love arrives on two
And four feet.

Barks and whistles and purrs
Filling our homes
With feathers and fur.

They sit with us at dinner
Doesn't matter if were grumpy or sinners.

Rest on our laps, land on our heads,
Push us out of our comfortable beds.

Make us happier than alcohol, dope or drugs
Even if they sometimes soil the rug.

For a little food and a few simple toys
They fill our lives with endless joy.

Cold wet noses, whiskers and tweets

Love arrives on two
And four feet.

Forever Faithful

They come to us in many ways,
A rescue, a breeder, a stray that stays.
They enter our hearts and make us whole.
We give them our love.
They give us their souls.

For some our eyes, for others our ears.
They detect our cancers and give us more years.
Changing blood sugars and seizure activity
Not beyond their olfactory proclivities.

They stand with our soldiers in warfare
And give their lives with a courageous dare.
They find lost children and comfort the sad
Bearing witness through the good and the bad.

They visit our elders in their decline
And into nursing homes bring sunshine.
The first line responders into the rubble
They never retreat no matter the trouble.

Whether they talk, bark, meow or squeak
They should be honored every week.
Whether fur, feathers or scales
Their devotion to us never fails.

May we humans learn from our faithful pets
And give them lifelong love, compassion and respect.

Unleashed

Silent, slumped figures.
Faces creased by age.
Gnarled joints stiff and deformed.

He enters the zone of indifference.
Wrinkled countenances now smoothed by smiles.
Hands miraculously unfold to reach for his head.
Animated conversations about childhood pets.

He melts into each lap.
Then slides to the floor in ecstasy.
Laughter fills the dead space.

The awakenings unleashed by a therapy dog.

One More Moment

Your invisibleness touches my leg.
The warm softness of your tongue wets my fingers.
The gentle pressure of your paw against my foot.
I don't know where heaven is
Or where spirits dwell,
But your essence surrounds my body
And that long desired
Just one more moment
Seems, oh, so close today.
Then you vanish into the ethers
As quickly as you came.
Leaving me knowing that,
One more moment
Would never be enough.

A Dog's Prayer

When the time comes that I must go
Hold me in your arms just so.

Hold me close to your loving heart
In quiet peace let me depart.

Let me gaze upon your tear stained face.
One last breath, one final embrace.

With a final wag, I bid good-by
In your gentle arms, I quietly died.

Bonded beyond this life by grace.
Don't forget my loving face.

Norman

In memoriam November 16, 2014

Come...
You never disobey that command.

Come...
There is always a treat and a hug.

Come...
You must be distracted by some enticing scent.

Come...
You must be swimming with the geese.

Come...
With a hopeful heart, I catch a glimpse
As you disappear
Across the pond into the haze beyond the sunlight.

My voice silenced by sadness.
You don't turn back.
You never come again.

Leaping Lab

Licking, leaping, lapping machine.
Agile, able acrobatic ace.
Frolicking, frivolous, fractious fiend.
Limping, lumbering, lovable lab.
Pouting, pugnacious, precious pal.
Jovial, jumping, joyous jester.
Noble, nifty, natural – Norman

A fine filament of fur
Woven into the Velcro on my jacket
----- my dog rises from the dead.

A Tropical Suite

Warm waves undulate beneath my hands.
Heat and brightness of a mid-day tropical sun.
A calypso beat from Jimmy Buffet's Margheritaville.
The hint of saline rising from the water.
My fingers tremble uncontrollably.

The patient small and fragile rests on the heat blanket.
Tubes and wires like seaweed entangle the life form,
Basking on the beach,
Unaware of danger.

A deep breath anchors me to the moment.
There can be no mistakes here.
No unsteady hands.
No back up surgeon.
No blood bank.
One unskillful cut—
Death is certain.

The sun moves toward the patient.
Light rising over the surgical field.
Rock steady hands slice into the skin.

The Back Window

A four karat diamond and
professionally manicured nails,
belie her teary claim
she couldn't afford Fluffy's care.
The loud tapping of the receptionist's pen,
Morse code for you've been had.
The shadow of the Mercedes hood ornament
projected onto the waiting room wall.
Fluffy's soulful eyes plead, "help me."

The sigh of the technician translates to
She's giving away the ranch,
as she places the IV catheter.
The stern, scolding hands on hips hospital manager
"we have bills to pay."

At day's end Fluffy is placed in the hands
With the four karat diamond and luxury car keys.
Tires squeal as the car speeds from the parking lot.
Fluffy's grateful brown eyes stare from the rapidly
Disappearing back window.

Good Grief!

No, no, no I'm not ready for him to be dead.
I'm sorry, his injuries were too extensive.
No, we play each morning.
He rides on the handle of the shopping cart.
He commandeers the vacuum during house cleaning.
I can't go on without him.

Between body heaving sobs she breathes into his nostrils.
No, Sage come back!
You must not give up on him.
There's nothing I can do. He's dead.

From the waiting room the muffled cries of a son,
Who crushed his mother's bird.
An hour and half later she leaves.
The lifeless pile of feathers on the bereavement room couch.

I'm calling to see how you all are doing after last night.
Oh, doctor, thanks for all your help.

We just got another bird.

A Precious Gift

Human and animal hearts forever entwined.
This is truly a gift divine.
When their bodies from this earth depart
They leave behind their loving heart.
Such grief and loss we could not abide
If they did not leave something behind.

At a special place their animal souls wait
Until their human enters that gait.
Souls and hearts joined in delight
Forever together in eternal light.

Queen of Agility

There is no other with her ability.
She is the queen of agility.
Over the jumps she glides with ease.
More skill than the man on the flying trapeze.

When she wiggles through the weaves,
My boy dog senses almost take leave.
Into the tunnel she disappears
My longing heart stills in fear.
Only to dance and sing with delight
When she appears back in sight.

Over the dog walk she saunters with pride
Oh, what a graceful stride.
To the end of the course her body sways.
Oh, if with her I could have my way.

For me there will be no other
With boy dog kisses I will smother
The queen I want to make a mother.

Killing Field

The heaviness settled.
We sat in silence.
Sadness trumped the exhaustion.
Molly, Lily, Paxton and Jack.
Hours earlier family pets,
Now carcasses in the killing field.

A service dog dead long before his time.
The barred hen feld by a complicated surgery.
The golden retriever paralyzed in a nanosecond.
The geriatric cockatiel ravished by cancer.

Grief unleashed, bond severed,
Laid waste by human hands.
What do I know of healing
Sitting in the killing field.

Eleanor

Pitter, patter, squawk, squawk.
Head held high and then it's cocked.

Preening plants and flinging seeds.
What is the next mischievous deed?

Sleeping dog—she'll end that dream.
A peck on the nose and a dastardly scream.

Uncovered toes a special delight.
Human rising in unmitigated fright.

A lunch break on books and wooden treasures
No bird could image such unfetted pleasures.

Remodeling cabinets an afternoon chore.
Maybe tonight a redesigned door.

The sun has set her work complete.
Upon my lap she rests her feet.

An exhausted chirp from a feathered fiend.
My home----

A nest box for a cockatiel queen.

Testosterone Serenade

NO ONE.......... Greets the day like a rooster.
Calling that small sliver on the horizon
Into full blistering bloom.

His pride on parade.
His fierce serenade.

The cock of the walk.
His testosterone talk.

He bedazzles his harem.
The predators, well, he just scares 'em.

Bounding sounds echo around.
Banishing him from many a town.

He doesn't care.
His message clear.
He's a majestic Chanticleer.

Dudley

His ashen face carved by grief,
Partially hidden by the gray hood
Containing his sorrow.
Her limp body draped across his arms.

The words of this landscape are silence and tears.
To intrude would be unholy.
Cliches of meaningless phrases- I'm sorry for your loss,
Would give no solace to sorrow so profound.

His hulking figure reduced to smallness in
Death's unforgiving grasp.
Tear swollen eyes search for answers
Where none are possible.

For twenty-four hours he has held her.
In silence he extends his arms toward me
And relinguishes her lifeless form,
As a folded wing escapes from beneath the shroud.

Breathless

Under the spell of Priestly's magic potions,
A sleeping beauty, hovering between life and death
The gentle uplifting of her sternum –
                    The only measure of life.

Levitated on a heated air mattress.
Wires measuring the waveforms of life,
Entangle her three-ounce frame.

The quiver of her feathers
Match the quiver of my hands
Cutting through the taut thin skin.

Holding my breath,
I guide microsurgical instruments
Around blood vessels and organs.

The ominous ovum
Delivered fragment by fragment.
Crushed organs now flush with blood.

The Doppler registers a strong steady pulse.
The last suture placed,
I begin to breathe again.

The Incredible Egg

Umbrella, Bared eyed, Red vented, Goffin, Moluccan, Ledbetter
Palm, Gang gang, Rose breasted, Citron, Eleanora.
Toco, Keel billed, Aracari, White throated, Crimson rumped
Sulphur breasted, Curl crested.
Blue and Gold, Scarlet, Hyacinth, Red fronted, Catalina, Spix
Blue throated, Military, Severe, Hahn'a, Yellow collared.
Blue front, Yellow nape, Red lore, Orange wing,
White front, Mealy, Panama, Cuban, Hispanolian,
Festive, Tucuman, Red spectacle, Lilac crown.
Sandhill, Whooping, Red crown, White nape, Wattle.
Lutino, Pied, Silver face, Olive, Cinnamon, Pearl.
Gouldian, Society, Zebra, Owl, Cut throat, Diamond,
Mannikan, Strawberry, Tiger, Java Rice and Spice.
Chicken.

Huntress

Craigy angular contracted form.
Huntress of the marsh
Expanding into sculptured, graceful curves,
Pursuing subterranean, sluggish silhouettes
Cooled by the rising Autumn sun.

Stiletto beak spears the prey.
Quivering muscular legs
Silently disappear into the digestive juices
Only to reappear in the heron's excrement
In the mud.

Splash Down

A splash down even Houston would applaud.
No heat shield.
No parachute.
Precise coordinates.
Exact date.

Feathered cargo planes,
Landing gear accurately angled,
Skillfully skimming, gliding and sliding
Across the recently thawed runway.
Barely perceptible ripples arising
To awaken the frosted marsh.
Spring touches down on Bellevue Pond.

A Cat's Prayer

Let me rest upon your soft, warm lap.
Where I enjoyed my afternoon naps.

Gently caress my head in your hands
That always patted me on demand.

Let my fur hold your abundant tears
As we reminisce all the years.

When the injection stills my heart
Embraced by your love I will depart.

Our broken hearts will finally mend
When we join again in the eternal end.

Yesterday's Favorite

She slithers around my legs
As I stumble toward the frig.
Her unspoken demand almost realized.

Her tail raised in ecstasy.
The deafening crescendos of meows and yeows.
Breakfast served on her favorite dish.

The tail drops.
Ears flatten
Silence.

She buries the food with imaginary dirt.
and saunters away.
Clearly conveying that was yesterday's favorite.

Unforgiven

At two A.M. her purr arrives.
She sits on my head
And stares into my eyes.
She kneads on my body and purrs even louder.
I know you want the left-over chowder.

Gently placed upon the floor,
Indignantly she storms out the door.
This slight will surely go unforgiven
Even with an act of contrition.

Across the room she sits with a smirk.
I know the special surprise just lurks.
The soft squish between my toes
Now the burial ground for the hunted vole.

She turns her head and sways away.
The dawning of a fabulous cat day.

The Roar

A single howl announces the star
Not an angel nor kings from afar.

Crescendo rising in sacred sound
Tis the call of heaven's hound.

Choirs of angels silent in awe
The voice of God transmitted by paws.

Lioness roars in birth's labor pains
Answering the howl's sweet refrain.

Animals speak in sacred verse
While humankind destroys the earth.

Solstice night the earth sings strong
How did we humans go so wrong?

Darkest night of reborn light
Bless the species that got it right.

Sacred night, sounds of joy
The lioness' cub was –oops- not a boy.

The Bark of Redemption

Angry men eviscerate the earth.
To hatred and terror their actions give birth.
Global and galactal devastation of treasures
For mankind's destruction there are no measures.

Hearts fossilized with rage and pain.
This is what we humans call sane?

Bombs burst over Nativity Square
Mocking the sacred with dread and fear.
The world in silence stillness waits
Annihilation by some terrorist from Kuwait.

Seasonal caroles sing of redemption
Has the planet earth claimed an exemption?

Spawned without the sperm of man
Born of a virgin surrounded by lambs.
Untainted by the genome of hate
Animals are the solstice saints.

The lesson of the goddess gone male
The greatest saints are born with tails.

Celestial chorus of missiles and screams
Is this what the child redeemed?
So to the earth shrouded in dark
The voice of redemption is a warm friendly bark.

Solstice Storm

Safe and quiet the path we walk
Listening only to snowflakes talk.

Paw prints, human prints iced in form
Slowly erased in the winter storm.

The silent play of woodland critters
Whiteness beautifies human litter.

Whirring machined silenced by snow
Caring eye contact and a friendly hello.

A world stoned cold on techno speed
Not much time for a kindly deed.

Two shadows fade in the waning light
Joined in the darkness of solstice night.

Shadow and light the genesis twins
Snow makes pure the cosmic sin.

Grayness to blackness, darkness be gone.
The Light of the universe eternally born.

Buxom bearer of beguiling beauty.
Bees bow before your brilliance.
Burgeoning birther of blossoms –
The bodacious bud!

The Queen With No Crown
The day the circus elephants were freed

Her multi-ton body clumsily balances on the circular pedestal.
The fake jewel studded tiara secured to her enormous frontal bones.
The Greatest Show On Earth emblazoned on the top.

The smooth linear curve of her ivory tusks
Frame the serpiginous, wrinkled, flexible trunk.
Her giant soulful eyes hold the sadness of her captivity.

On command, she carefully dismounts and sits on her haunches.
Her large, leathery, gray ears flapping to the applause.
Then she rises on all four legs.

With her powerful trunk, she rips the crown from her head
And crushes it to the dust.
Today she bows to no one.

Today she is truly a queen with no crown.
Today she is free.
Today she is the Matriarch of her herd.

The Sounds of Silence
For Cecil

The humming and drumming hive alive.
The unwitnessed collapse.
The pollinators die.
The waggle dance done.
Winged striped carcasses burnt in the sun.

The whirling and twirling of the turbines.
The unheard crack of a broken back.
The eagle's painful silent descent.
Soaring done.
Broken body in the sun.

Walking and stalking on the plains.
The savannah breeze moving his mane.
Beheaded by the cowardly hunter.
Roaring done.
Eviscerated heart decaying in the sun.

Meat

An oozing slab of raw flesh
Carved from the flank of a contentedly grazing steer,
Still bleeding into the white styrofoam half casket
Sealed in clear plastic.
The tenderness and cut visible for evaluation,
Laced with chemicals to enhance the redness
Whetting our carnivore appetite for blood and meat.
Once fasiculating muscle fibers
Now stilled in the cool display case morgue
Stretched across the back wall of the grocery store.

Casually filling our shopping carts
With labeled and identified body parts
Hooves, bones, tongues, ribs, muscle
Brains, livers, pancreases and tripe.
Engaged in neighborly conversations
Condemning Isis beheadings.
Wondering when the violence will end,
As we shop each day at the morgue.

Where Do I Live?

In the soft pine needles carpeting the forest floor.
In the heart of an eagle that silently soars.

In the majestic trees dappled with birds.
In the open spaces that never need words.

In the effervescence of a sparkling wine.
In the endless embrace of the mysterious divine.

In the fierce caress of all that I love.
In the infinite galaxies streaming above.

In Gaia's sad and muffled groans.
In the universal sound that calls me home.

In the rainbow energy of the charka wheels.
In the hope of an earth finally healed.

In the cosmic field of the Creatrix' grid.
In the blessed mystery.....
                    that's where I live.

Poet's Biography

Dr. Marjorie McMillan grew up in a suburb of Boston, attended Northeastern University and graduated Summa Cum Laude from the Ohio State University College of Veterinary Medicine. She did an internship at Angell Animal Medical Center and eventually was department head of radiology after extensive post-doctoral training.

When she requested equal pay for equal work, after she found out her salary was significantly lower than the male department heads at Angell, she was given 15 minutes to vacate her office while she had a patient under anesthesia. Her successful lawsuit against MSPCA/Angell was one of the most important employment discrimination cases of the 1990's and changed case law.

Her interest in poetry was stimulated by her high school English teacher, Sister Mary Roberta, SSND, who was a Hopkins scholar. She named her veterinary hospital, The Windhover Veterinary Center, after the Hopkins poem.

Poetry allows her to pay tribute to her many patients and process the sad, difficult and joyful emotions that are all part of practicing veterinary medicine.

Acknowledgement

Thanks to the members of my poetry group: Kathy Leydon-Conway, Irene Hannigan, Joe Lawlor, Lisa Moncevicz, and Jan Slepian for their camaraderie, creativity and inspiration and our group leader, Jesse Brown, teacher extraordinaire, who always finds the positive in our work and whose encouraging words support us in our endeavors.

A special thank you to Tom Mournighan and Cathy Symons for their technical support and Joan Powers for her photography and cover design. Without their help, this book would not have been possible.

Made in the USA
Columbia, SC
09 October 2017